Finding the Right Container

Anne Montgomery

Smithsonian

buttons

Where should you
put them?

shoes

Where should you
put them?

tools

Where should you
put them?

cookies

Where should you
put them?

spoons

Where should you
put them?

eggs

Where should you
put them?

pencils

Where should you
put them?

toys

Where should you
put them?

The Problem

Your teacher has too many paper clips. They need a container.

The Goals

- Your container should hold 25 paper clips.
- It should be made of plastic building blocks.
- It should be easy to grab the paper clips.

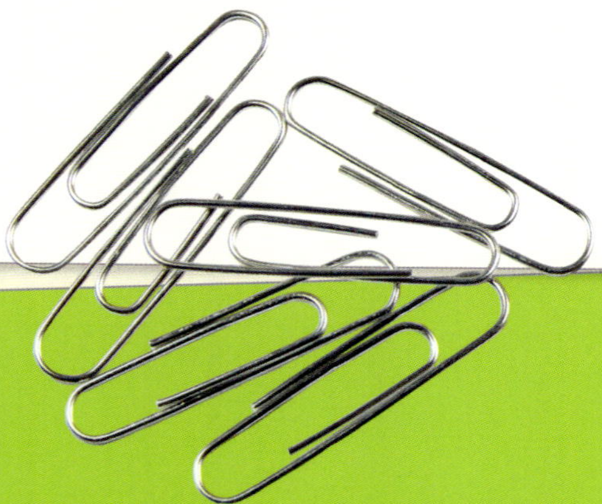

Research and Brainstorm

Learn about containers.

Design and Build

Draw your plan. Build your container!

Test and Improve

Place the paper clips in your container. Then, try to make it better.

Reflect and Share

What did you learn?

Consultants

Amy Zoque
STEM Coordinator and Instructional Coach
Vineyard STEM School
Ontario Montclair District

Siobhan Simmons
Marblehead Elementary
Capistrano Unified School District

Publishing Credits

Rachelle Cracchiolo, M.S.Ed., *Publisher*
Conni Medina, M.A.Ed., *Editor in Chief*
Diana Kenney, M.A.Ed., NBCT, *Series Developer*
Emily R. Smith, M.A.Ed., *Content Director*
Véronique Bos, *Creative Director*
Robin Erickson, *Art Director*
Stephanie Bernard, *Associate Editor*
Mindy Duits, *Senior Graphic Designer*
Smithsonian Science Education Center

Image Credits: all images from Shutterstock and/or iStock.

Library of Congress Cataloging-in-Publication Data
Names: Montgomery, Anne (Anne Diana), author. | Smithsonian Institution, contributor.
Title: Finding the right container / Anne Montgomery.
Description: Huntington Beach, CA : Teacher Created Materials, Inc., [2019] | "Smithsonian Institution"--Copyright statement. | Audience: Age 5. | Audience: K to grade 3. |
Identifiers: LCCN 2018055265 (print) | LCCN 2018057400 (ebook) | ISBN 9781425859855 (eBook) | ISBN 9781493866403 (pbk.)
Subjects: LCSH: Size perception--Juvenile literature. | Containers--Juvenile literature.
Classification: LCC BF299.S5 (ebook) | LCC BF299.S5 M66 2019 (print) | DDC 153.7/52--dc23
LC record available at https://lccn.loc.gov/2018055265

Smithsonian

Teacher Created Materials

5301 Oceanus Drive
Huntington Beach, CA 92649-1030
www.tcmpub.com
ISBN 978-1-4938-6640-3
© 2019 Teacher Created Materials, Inc.
Printed in China
51497